GILES & BUNNETT'S

VICTORIAN ARMY UNIFORM ALBUM

1888

GILES & BUNNETT'S

VICTORIAN ARMY UNIFORM ALBUM

1888

The Naval & Military Press

Published by

The Naval & Military Press Ltd
Unit 5 Riverside, Brambleside
Bellbrook Industrial Estate
Uckfield, East Sussex
TN22 1QQ England

Tel: +44 (0)1825 749494

www.naval-military-press.com
www.nmarchive.com

In reprinting in facsimile from the original, any imperfections are inevitably reproduced and the quality may fall short of modern type and cartographic standards.

Her Majesty's Army

THE HORSE GUARDS.

VOL. I.

HER MAJESTY'S ARMY

With Coloured Illustrations by G. D. Giles

VOLUME 1

LIST OF ILLUSTRATIONS.

VOL. I.

The Scots Guards

The Horse Guards

The 1st Life Guards

The 1st (Royal) Dragoons

The 10th (Prince of Wales's Own Royal) Hussars

The 16th (Queen's) Lancers

The Royal Artillery

The Royal Horse Artillery

The Royal Engineers

A Military Doctor

The 79th—Queen's Own Cameron Highlanders

A Chelsea Pensioner

The 68th—Durham Light Infantry

The 87th—Princess Victoria's (Royal Irish Fusiliers)

The 25th—King's Own Scottish Borderers

The 30th—East Lancashire

THE "SCOTS GUARDS."

THE 1st LIFE GUARDS.

1st (ROYAL) DRAGOONS.

THE 10th (PRINCE OF WALES' OWN ROYAL) HUSSARS.

THE 16th (QUEEN'S) LANCERS.

THE ROYAL ARTILLERY.

THE "ROYAL HORSE ARTILLERY."

ROYAL ENGINEERS.

A MILITARY DOCTOR.

The 79th QUEEN'S OWN CAMERON HIGHLANDERS.

A CHELSEA PENSIONER.

THE 68th—DURHAM LIGHT INFANTRY.

THE 87th—PRINCESS VICTORIA'S (ROYAL IRISH FUSILIERS).

THE 25th—KING'S OWN SCOTTISH BORDERERS

The 30th—EAST LANCASHIRE.

Her Majesty's Army

THE 24th SOUTH WALES BORDERERS.

VOL. II.

HER MAJESTY'S ARMY

With Coloured Illustrations by G. D. Giles

VOLUME 2

LIST OF ILLUSTRATIONS.

VOL. II.

The Honourable Artillery Company (Cavalry)

The 24th—South Wales Borderers

The 57th—Duke of Cambridge's Own (Middlesex)

The 43rd—Oxfordshire Light Infantry

The 42nd—The Black Watch (Royal Highlanders)

The 21st—Royal Scots Fusiliers

The 72nd—Seaforth Highlanders

The 2nd—Queen's (Royal West Surrey)

The 35th—Royal Sussex

The 23rd—Royal Welsh Fusiliers

The 15th—East Yorkshire

The Queen's Own Royal (Staffordshire Yeomanry)

The 1st Middlesex (Victoria Rifles)

The 7th Middlesex (The London Scottish)

The 20th Middlesex (Artists')

THE HONOURABLE ARTILLERY COMPANY.

(CAVALRY.)

THE 57th—DUKE OF CAMBRIDGE'S OWN (MIDDLESEX).

THE 43rd—OXFORDSHIRE LIGHT INFANTRY.

THE 42nd—THE BLACK WATCH (ROYAL HIGHLANDERS)

THE 21st—ROYAL SCOTS FUSILIERS.

THE 72nd--SEAFORTH HIGHLANDERS.

THE 2nd—THE QUEEN'S (ROYAL WEST SURREY).

THE 35th—ROYAL SUSSEX.

THE 23rd—ROYAL WELSH FUSILIERS.

THE 15th—EAST YORKSHIRE.

THE QUEEN'S OWN ROYAL REGIMENT.

STAFFORDSHIRE YEOMANRY.

THE 1st MIDDLESEX (VICTORIA RIFLES) VOLUNTEERS.

(4TH VOLUNTEER BATTALION KING'S ROYAL RIFLE CORPS.)

THE LONDON SCOTTISH
VOLUNTEERS.
(1st Volunteer Battalion Rifle Brigade), 7th Middlesex.

THE 20th MIDDLESEX (ARTISTS')
VOLUNTEERS.

Her Majesty's Indian and Colonial Forces

11th BENGAL NATIVE INFANTRY.

HER MAJESTY'S ARMY

INDIAN AND COLONIAL FORCES

With Coloured Illustrations

LIST OF ILLUSTRATIONS.

The Governor-General's Body Guard (Calcutta)

The 11th Bengal Native Infantry

The West India Regiment

The 13th Bengal Lancers

The 15th Sikhs

The 3rd Goorkhas

The 1st Madras Pioneers

The Bombay Artillery

The Halifax Garrison Artillery

The 6th Regiment of Cavalry (Hussars, Canada)

The 2nd Queen's Own Rifles (Canada)

The 5th Royal Scots of Canada (Montreal)

The Cape Mounted Rifles

The 1st Battalion (West Melbourne) Victoria Infantry

The Victorian Mounted Rifles

The Victorian Artillery

THE GOVERNOR-GENERAL'S BODY-GUARD,
CALCUTTA.

WEST INDIA REGIMENT.

THE 13th BENGAL LANCERS.

15th SIKHS.

THE 3rd GOORKHAS.

FIRST MADRAS PIONEERS.

THE BOMBAY ARTILLERY.

HALIFAX GARRISON ARTILLERY.

THE 6th REGIMENT OF CAVALRY (HUSSARS, CANADA).

THE 2nd QUEEN'S OWN RIFLES (CANADA).

THE 5th ROYAL SCOTS OF CANADA,

MONTREAL.

THE CAPE MOUNTED RIFLES.

1st BATTALION (WEST MELBOURNE) VICTORIAN INFANTRY.

VICTORIAN MOUNTED RIFLES.

VICTORIAN ARTILLERY.

www.ingramcontent.com/pod-product-compliance
Lightning Source LLC
Chambersburg PA
CBHW060926170426
43192CB00025B/2903